Build-a-Skill Instant Books

R-Controlled Vowels and Vowel Digraphs

Written by
Kim Cernek

Editors: Vicky Shiotsu and Stacey Faulkner
Illustrators: Jenny Campbell and Darcy Tom
Cover Illustrator: Rick Grayson
Designer: The Development Source
Art Director: Moonhee Pak
Project Director: Betsy Morris

Printed in China through Colorcraft Ltd., Hong Kong

Table of Contents

Instant Books

Introduction

About the Build-a-Skill Instant Books Series

The *Build-a-Skill Instant Books* series features a variety of reproducible instant books that focus on important reading and math skills covered in the primary classroom. Each instant book is easy to make, and once children become familiar with the basic formats that appear throughout the series, they will be able to make new books with little help. Children will love the unique, manipulative quality of the books and will want to read them over and over again as they gain mastery of basic learning skills!

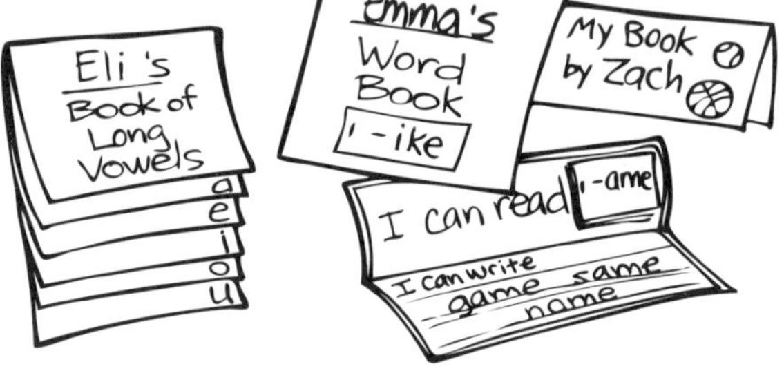

About the Build-a-Skill Instant Books: R-Controlled Vowels and Vowel Digraphs

This book features the five r-controlled vowels and common vowel digraphs in fun and easy-to-make instant books. Children will develop fine motor skills and practice following directions as they cut, fold, and staple the reproducible pages together to make flip books, shape books, word wallets, and more! As children read and reread their instant books, they will strengthen their decoding skills and increase their sight word vocabulary.

Refer to the Table of Contents to help with lesson planning. Choose instant book activities that fit with the curriculum goals in your regular or ELL classroom. Use the instant books to practice skills or introduce new ones. Directions for making the instant books appear on pages 3 and 4. These should be copied and sent along with the book patterns when assigning a bookmaking activity as homework.

Making and Using the Instant Books

All of the instant books in this resource require only one or two pieces of paper. Copy the pages on white copy paper or card stock, or use colored paper to jazz up and vary the formats. Children will love personalizing their instant books by coloring them, adding construction paper covers, or decorating them with collage materials such as wiggly eyes, ribbon, and stickers. Customize the instant books by creating your own word cards using the reproducible on page 32.

Children can make instant books as an enrichment activity when their regular classwork is done, as a learning center activity during guided reading time, or as a homework assignment. They can place completed instant books in their classroom book boxes and then read and reread the books independently or with a reading buddy. After children have had many opportunities to read their books in school, send the books home for extra skill-building practice. Encourage children to store the books in a special box that they have labeled "I Can Read Box."

Directions for Making the Instant Books

There are five basic formats for the instant books in this guide. The directions appear below for quick and easy reference. The directions are written *to* the child, in case you would like to send the bookmaking activities home as homework. Just copy the directions and attach them to the instant book pages.

Flip Book, pages 5, 8, 11, 14, 17

1. Finish the book by tracing the dotted letters.
2. Cut out the flip book and word cards.
3. Staple the cards to the flip book.
4. "Flip up" each card to practice reading your words.

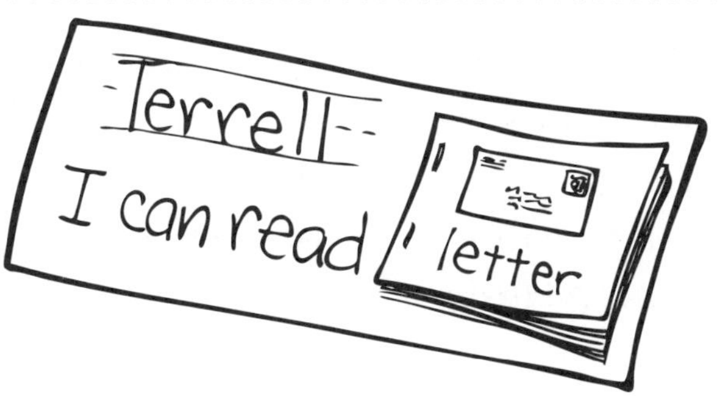

Strip Book, pages 6–7, 9–10, 12–13, 15–16, 18–19

1. Finish the book by tracing the dotted words.
2. Cut out the strips.
3. Put the strips in order. Staple them on the left.

Optional: Make and decorate a construction paper cover, and color the pictures.

Shape Book, pages 20, 21, 22, 23, 24, 25

1. Trace the dotted letters on each word card.
2. Cut out the shape and the word cards.
3. Staple the word cards to the shape.
4. Practice reading your words!

Word Wallet, pages 26–27, 28–29

1. Trace the dotted letters on the wallet.
2. Cut out the wallet.
3. Fold it in half along the solid middle line.
4. Staple where shown. Tape the outer edges. Fold the wallet closed.
5. Cut out the word cards. Sort them into the correct pockets.

Read-and-Write Book, pages 30–31

1. Cut out the read-and-write book.
2. Glue it to a piece of construction paper the same size.
3. Cut out the word cards. Staple them to the top strip.
4. Practice writing your words below.
5. Fold the book in half and decorate the cover.

Optional: Add extra writing paper.

ar

Flip Book

I can read

Staple word cards here.

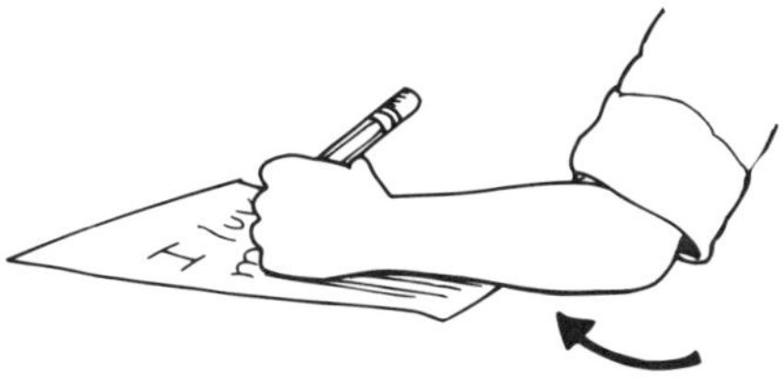

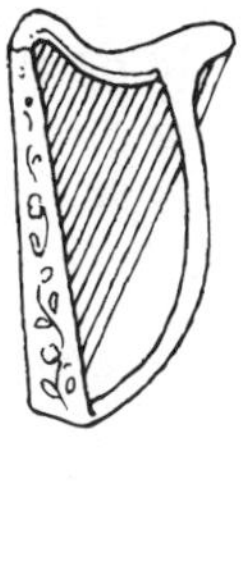

arm	barn	farm
harp	jar	star

The Water Park Strip Book

The Water Park

by ____________________

1

It's eight o'clock sharp.

2

Let's start the car.

3

The Water Park Strip Book

er

Flip Book

I can read

Staple word cards here.

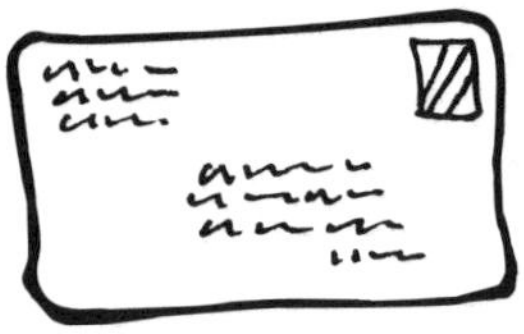 letter	 finger	butter
 zipper	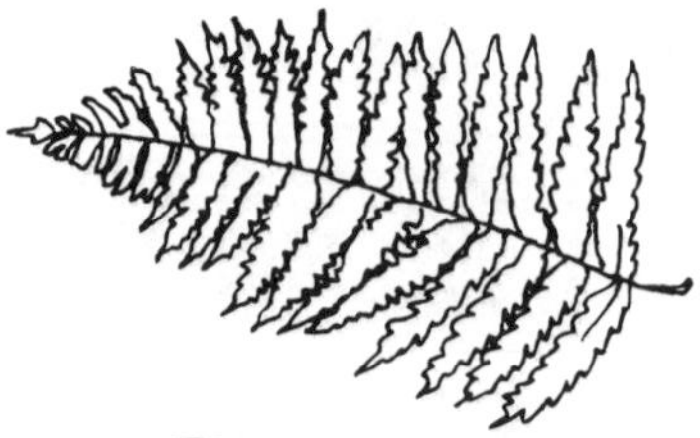 fern	river

My Diner Strip Book

______________'s

Diner

1

My mother is the baker.

2

My father is her helper.

3

My Diner Strip Book

My brother is the waiter.

4

I am the owner.

5

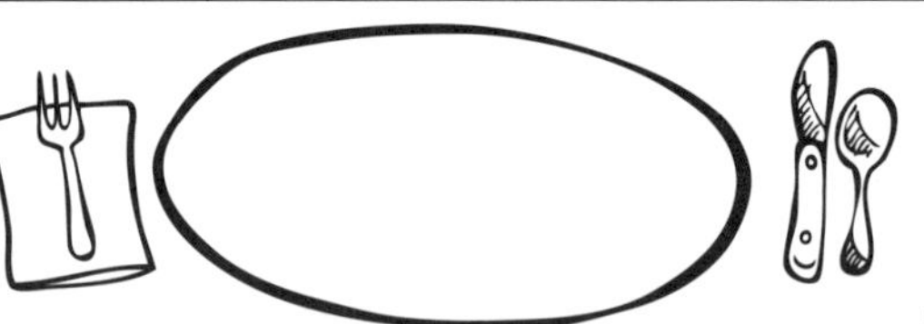

Welcome to my diner!
What would you like?

6

ir

Flip Book

I can read

Staple word cards here.

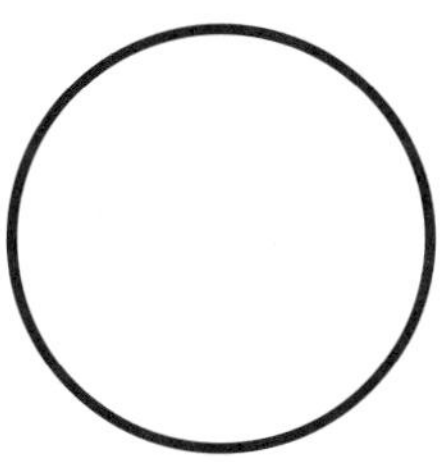

stir	bird	first
circle	dirt	fir

The Circus Strip Book

The Circus

by ______________

1

She put on a shirt.
She put on a skirt.

2

Then the girl put
a bow in her hair.

3

The Circus Strip Book

With a swirl
and a twirl

4

She danced
in a whirl

5

With the silly
old circus bear.

6

or

Flip Book

I can read

Staple word cards here.

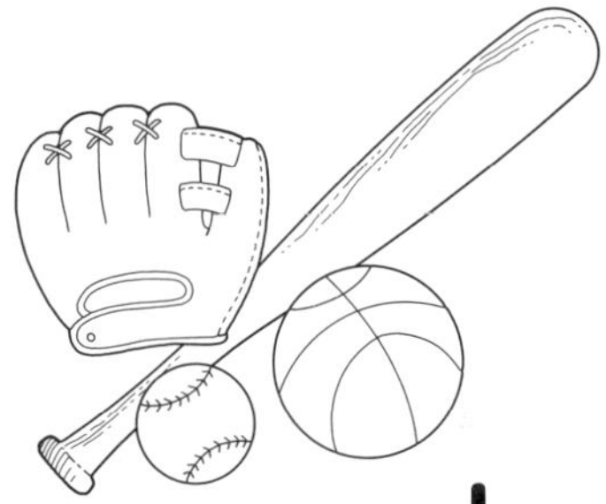

sport	stork	fork
fort	horn	thorn

A Horse Strip Book

A Horse

by ____________________

1

Early one morn,

a horse ate some corn

2

And went

for a ride to the west.

3

A Horse Strip Book

It rode by a porch 4

Where a man
with a torch 5

Thought a ride to the
north would be best. 6

ur

Flip Book

Staple word cards here.

I can read

 hurt	 nurse	 church
 purse	 burst	 curl

Surprise! Strip Book

Surprise!

by ______________

1

Brush your fur.

2

Put on a purple hat.

3

Surprise! Strip Book

ai **Shape Book**

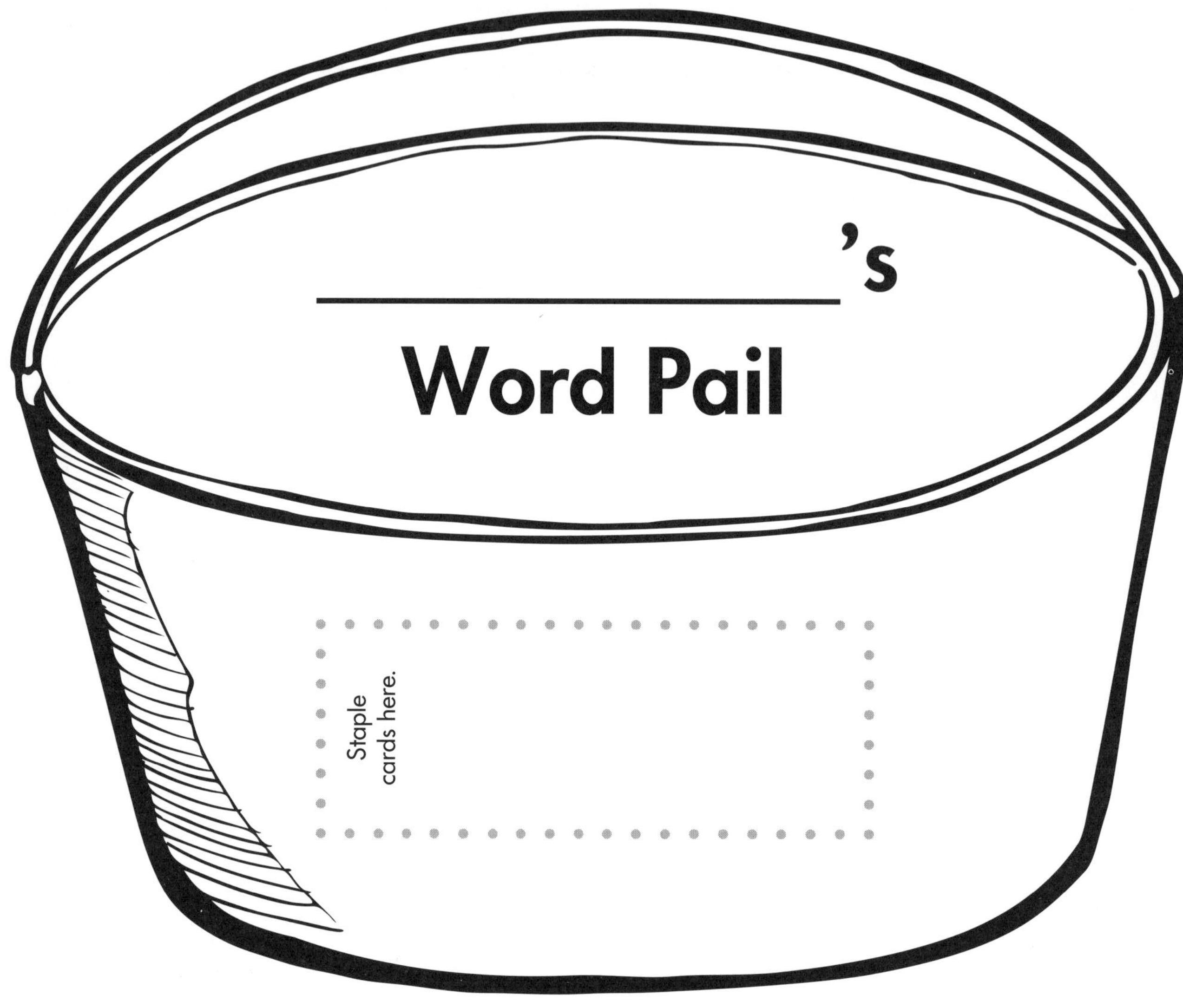

rain	wait
pail	tail
sail	pain

ay

Shape Book

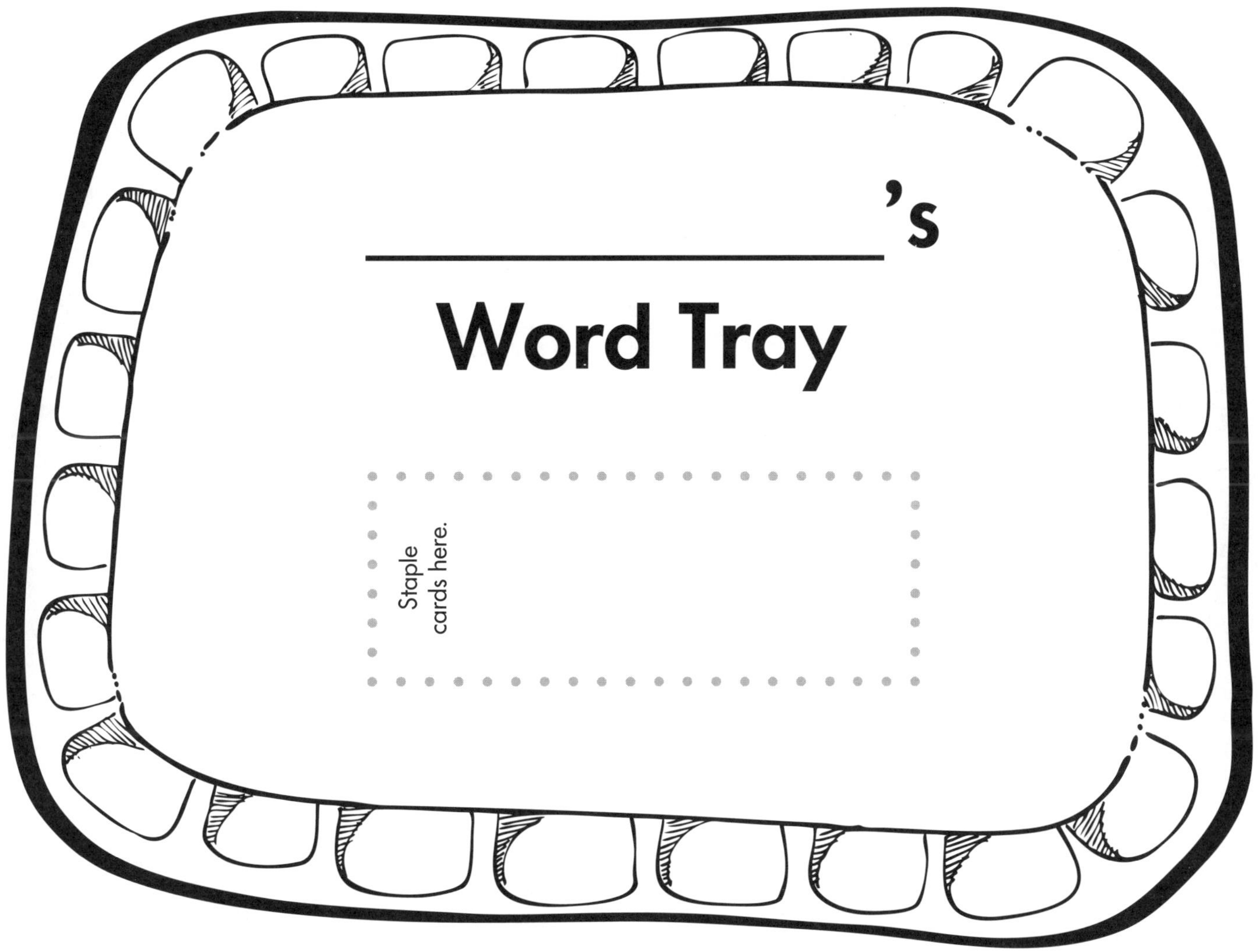

play	clay
pay	hay
May	say

oa Shape Book

soap	road
coat	loaf
goat	toad

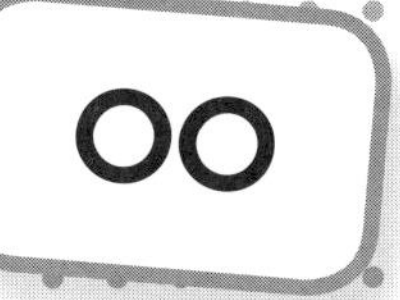

oo Shape Book

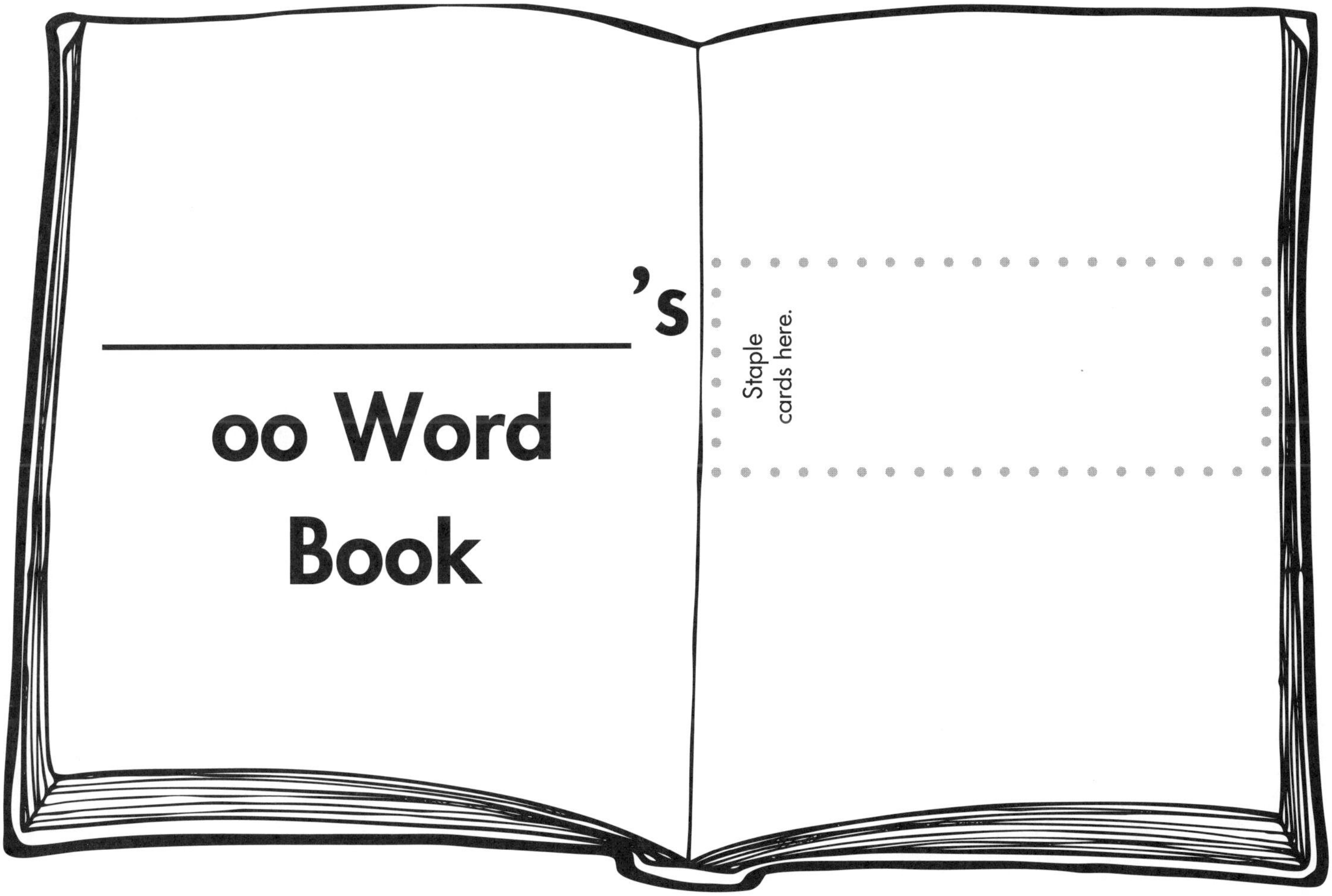

______________'s
oo Word Book
Staple cards here.

look 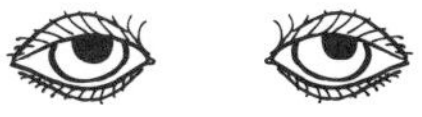	foot 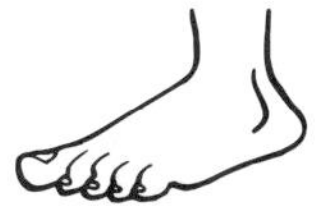
hood	hook 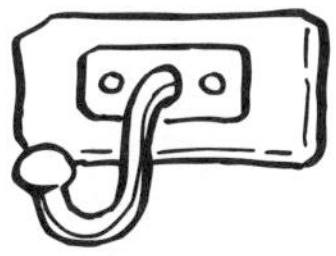
wood 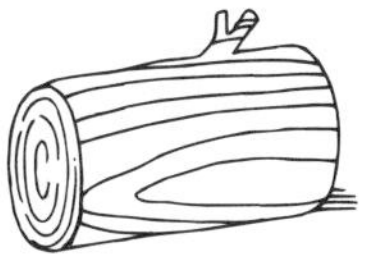	cook

oo

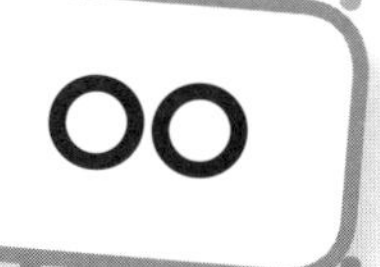

Shape Book

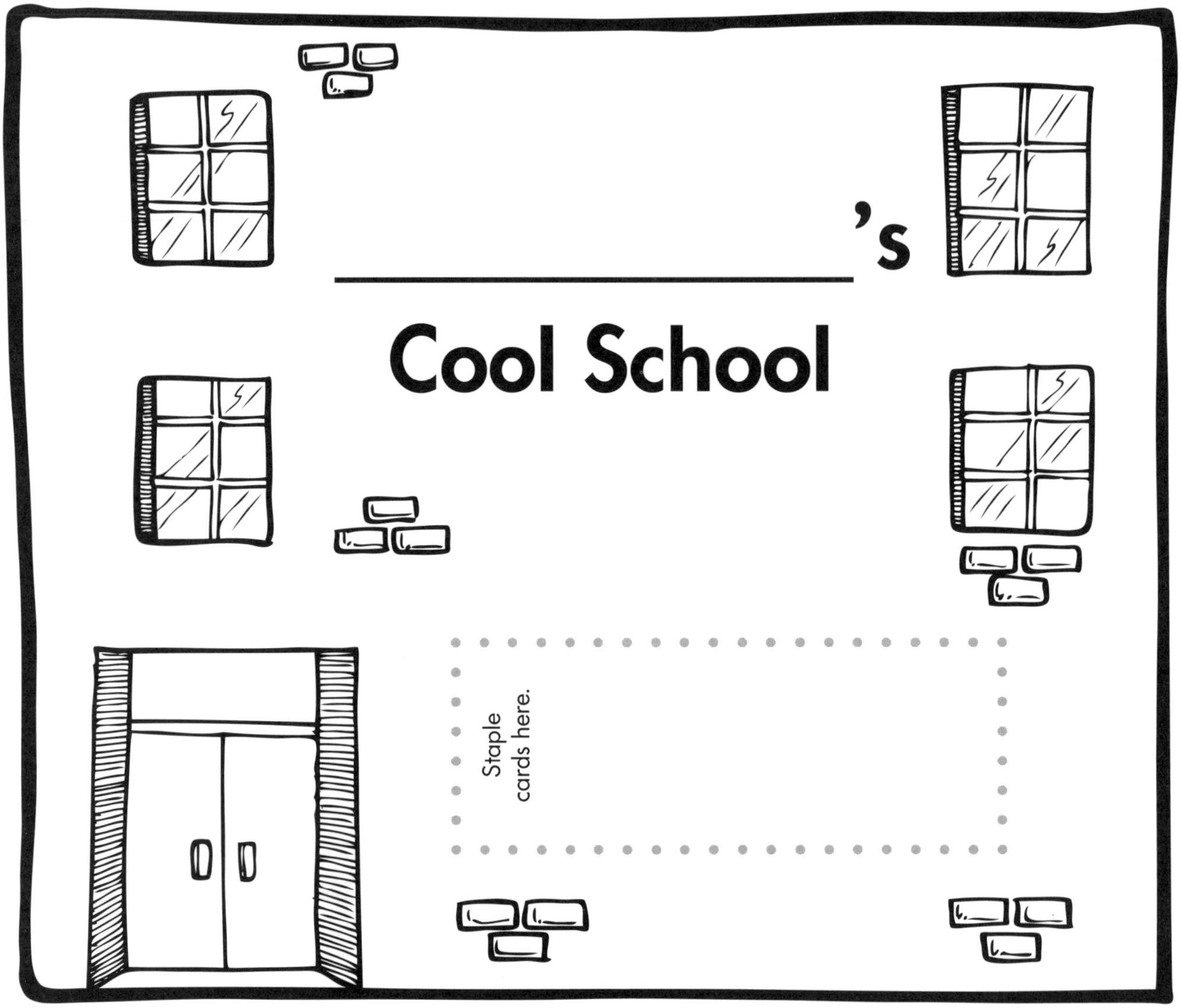

____________'s
Cool School
Staple cards here.

boot 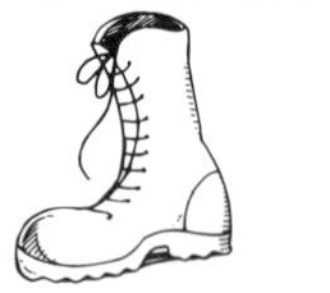	stool
broom	food 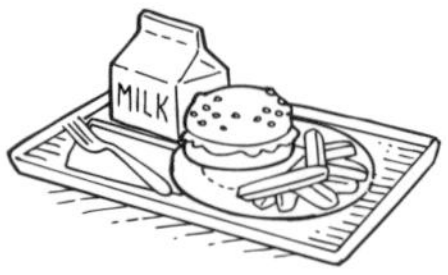
spoon 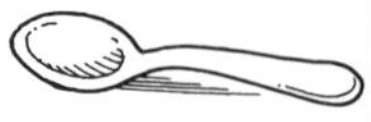	hoop

ow

Shape Book

bow	row
crow	bowl
blow	grow

ea, ee, ie

Word Wallet

ea

Words

leaf

ee

Words

tree

ie

Words

thief

Fold here.

Word Wallet

_______'s

Tape here.

Staple here.

Staple here.

Tape here.

Wallet Words

seal	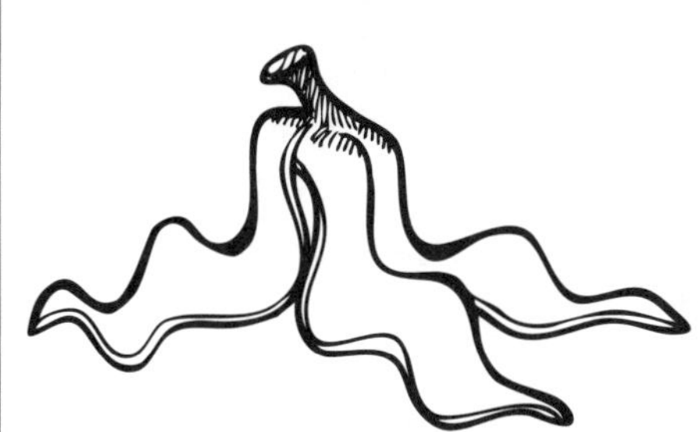 peel	 eat
 field	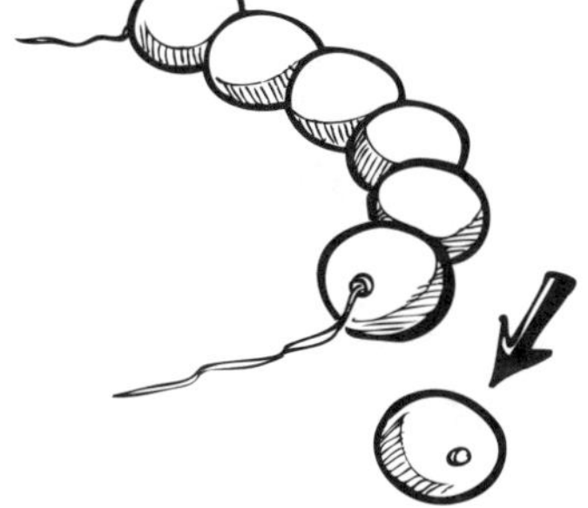 bead	 sleep
 shield	 wheel	 piece

oo, oo, ue

Word Wallet

oo

Words

book

oo

Words

school

ue

Words

glue

Fold here.

Word Wallet

______'s

Tape here.

Staple here.

Staple here.

Tape here.

oo, oo, ue

Wallet Words

took	room	tooth
blue	hoof	shook
clue	moon	true

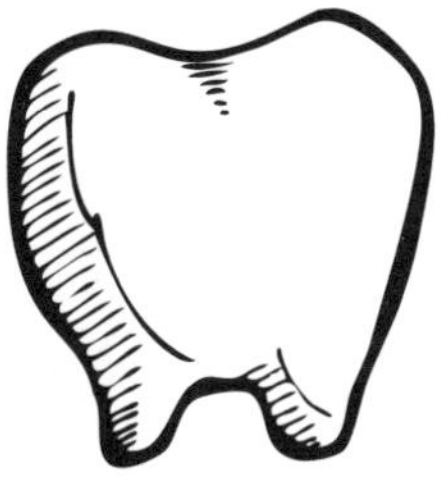

Read-and-Write Book

Staple word cards here.

I can read

I can write

ea

Word Cards

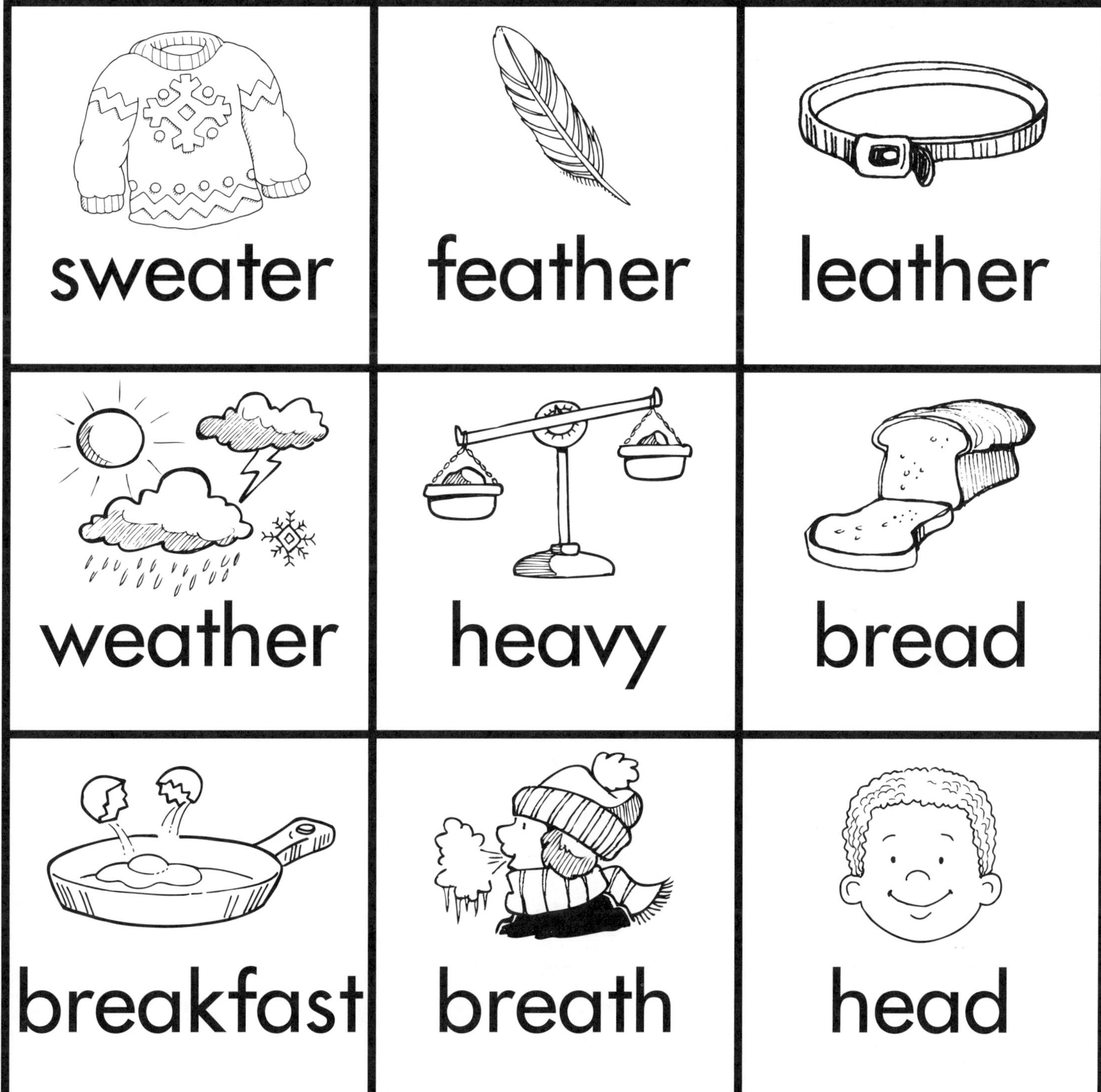

Make Your Own

Word Cards